TOWARDS A BETTER COUNTRY

A Quest For Visionary Leadership In Africa

A WaaGovernment Action Propelling Tool on Citizenship, Democratic Advancement, And Sustainable Development

Ledogo Amabu

Foreword

By

Tonye Cole, Mni.

Co-founder and former Group Executive Director of Sahara Group

i

The Series Three Of The Classic Book:

WAAGOVERNMENT AND THEORY OF NATIONS.

A Relationship Inspired Revolutionary Classic On Good Governance, Nationhood, Patriotism, Leadership, Development, And Social Change.

Contents

FOREWORD

When the author, Ledogo Amabu, contacted me to write a foreword to his classic, ***WaaGovernment & Theory of Nations***, I could not resist the drive, passion, and commitment to nation-building that his personality exudes. And to think that this daunting task was thrown at me at a time I was completely engrossed with party politics and electioneering activities, I would have had a legitimate excuse for shirking away from this responsibility. But I was willing to carry out the task because the inspiration of the author resonates with the vision of my own Foundation and the similar passion I have for the development of this great nation—Nigeria, as well as the African continent. I have also, in my personal capacity and through my foundation, mentored young people both on the African continent and globally along the lines of hard work, patriotism, and self-development. I, therefore, consider it a singular honor to have been asked to write this foreword.

The Book, ***WaaGovernment & Theory of Nations*** is written as a trilogy and arranged in series. Series One is entitled, '***The African Virgin For Change.***' This Series begins with an introduction of the female protagonist, '***WaaGovernment***'—the prefix 'Waa' being derived from the Khana dialect of Ogoni meaning 'a lovely woman in the life of a man in the position of trust, or an influential woman in the society seeking change in her country. Thus, it is with this ***WaaGovernment*** that the author struck a relationship that became a catalyst for the activities embedded in a subsequent series of the Book.

But *WaaGovernment* is more than a persona. It is also an ideology consummated in the unquenchable passion to see one's country in a positive light; to rise and defend the overall interest of one's country; a demonstrable unshakable commitment to the peace, development, and advancement of one's country; and above all, a call to extricate oneself from the constraining binds of ethnocentrism, nepotism, mediocrity, corruption, and selfishness, which are the banes of development in any society. With this ideology firmly entrenched in the leaders and the governed, the author believes that the moral decadence, mal-administration, corruption, underdevelopment, and other vices plaguing the African continent, and indeed Nigeria, will give way to a properly governed society where the aspirations of the vast majority of citizens will be met.

Series Two, which is entitled, *'Education: The Bedrock of Nation Building'* is remarkable for its rich blend of scholarship and research. In this series, the author admirably emphasizes in unmistakable terms the crucial role education plays and will continue to play in any quest for the development of Africa and indeed Nigeria. It is worthwhile to stress that this book is an eye-opener on the glaring shortfall in the standard of education required to unleash the potential of the African child towards making positive and measurable contributions towards nation-building. The author highlights the yawning gap in the curriculum operated in the African educational system and what is needed to educate the total African child to make him or her globally competitive. The series is the solution to all of Africa's problems through a well-rounded education that emancipates the mind and opens it up to limitless possibilities.

This series argues for a recalibration of the educational system and curriculum currently in use in Africa and advocates for a paradigm shift from a classroom and theory-based education to a more pragmatic, problem-solving, and result-oriented one. To achieve this level of education for both the boy and girl child, the author recommends a collaborative partnership between the government and critical private institutions and individuals. The author concludes that the government alone cannot provide all of the resources and reach required to bring education to all African children – including the poor, homeless, destitute, and those living with disabilities.

Series Three which is entitled, '***Towards a Better Country: A Quest for Visionary Leadership in Africa***' is devoted to a discourse on the important role of democratic governance and citizen's political participation in the development of a nation. In this Series, the author observes a disturbing trend where citizens shirk away from the political and electoral space for various reasons. With a focus on the 2023 general elections in Nigeria – and the Presidential and National Assembly elections held last Saturday, 25 February 2023 – with the results not fully announced days after the conclusion of polls, the author has zealously inspired the teeming youths of Nigeria and indeed the African continent to demonstrate their loyalty to their fatherland by taking a keen interest in the process that throws up their leaders. Akin to the adage that evil thrives where good people refuse to speak up, the author argues that the imposition of candidates by political parties and the imposition of public office holders are made possible when the citizens alienate themselves from election and political-related activities.

Furthermore, in Series Three, the author issues a clarion call to all citizens of Nigeria both within and in the diaspora to actively participate in this year's general elections and political activities in the country going forward. He challenges the citizens of Nigeria and Africa – young people and patriots – to realign our priorities and perspectives on the choice of leaders and leadership along the criteria of competence, capacity, and merit, rather than ethnicity and blind party loyalty.

Indeed, it cannot be gainsaid that the author has brilliantly established an inextricable link between the opening of the democratic space and citizens' active political participation, on the one hand, and good governance, on the other hand. The author's optimism of a better Nigeria and Africa needs to be commended and his demand for visionary leadership in all strata of governance is one to be taken very seriously if Africa is to become the *el dorado* we all dream about. As patriots of our great country and continent, we must demand principled leadership and management of our human and material resources anchored on responsibility, accountability, transparency, and probity. It is fascinating that the author emphasized the role of credibility and transparency in the electoral process in instilling confidence in the electorate and their concomitant mass participation in the electoral process. This point is strategic and the 2023 general elections in Nigeria will serve as a test case as to whether Nigeria is moving along the path of greatness so vigorously and passionately recommended by the author. The jury will be out soon!

I must state unequivocally, at this juncture, that Amabu is indeed a shining star – a bright spark on the African continent – a continent labeled as dark, not because of its paucity of human and natural resources, but for its leadership shortsightedness, greed, and avarice. Amabu's passion for nation-building as demonstrated in the pages of this Book and the recognition for meritorious services rendered for God and the country has proven that Africa can get it right if the citizens show enough patriotism, despite our glaring decades of underdevelopment. It is, therefore, expected that African leaders, governments, citizens, and institutions will utilize the valuable insights and lessons learned from this Book to re-invent the wheels of education, leadership, governance, and patriotism at all levels of our society. This will in turn drastically reduce, if not completely eradicate, corruption, ethnicism, nepotism, and leadership failure which have so monstrously blighted the development of Africa and prevented it for decades from assuming its pride of place in the comity of nations.

It is, therefore, against the foregoing conviction, that I have no hesitation in recommending this book to all Statesmen and women, members of the political class, young people, academics, students, and all those genuinely passionate about the development of Nigeria and the African continent and the greatness of its people. I certify that the Book is a must-read for anyone passionate about nation-building, patriotism, social change, leadership, self-development, and value for relationships.

Tonye Cole, Mni.

Co-founder and former Group Executive Director of Sahara Group

One

INTRODUCTION

Growing up, I loved reading news in National dailies. After I finished secondary school, I couldn't stay a single day without going to the vendor's stand. I would go through and read at list 4 dailies a day. I would search through pages and glance through several articles on self-development, politics, leadership, and governance. This really built a strong passion in me to become the change the society needed and to provide solutions to the plethora of challenges written about in the dailies.

In the course of this work, I came across an article in ThisDay Newspaper, a leading Nigerian national daily. The article was titled, "Shonekan and a country in search of a Sage."

In that article, the author wrote thus:

"Since independence in 1960, many problems have rocked Nigeria to its foundations, ruining the promise of a country that once held the priceless promise of becoming Africa's first world super power. From the first military coup in 1966 which precipitated a calamitous and precipitous civil war in 1967 to subsequent military coups, military regimes of dubious legacies, and Nigeria's struggles to enshrine accountable democracy since 1999. The giant of Africa has known rapid depreciation in the hands of those who would falter a giant."

After I read the article on The Search for a Sage in Nigeria, I was moved and began to think why, despite population advantage and our beautiful diversity, growth has been distorted in a promising country. I then understood that the major cause of the instability is that we have not been able to make considerable effort and patriotic attempts to come together and build the fragile country handed over to our founding fathers by the British in our collective desire and quest for a better country for the achievement of nationhood.

Many pre-independence and post-independence leaders were nationalistic thinkers. They could not think of building the country to achieve nationhood. They pursued nationalism instead of nationhood.

Nationhood is the building of a country to think and stay together with pride. In Nigeria, past leaders and successive governments have pursued nationalism instead of nationhood. It is the cause of Nigeria's backwardness and stunted growth since independence.

"A nation is a large number of people organized under a body of government and sharing common customs, origin, history or language'. But such a definition cannot go for a country like Nigeria with different languages, diverse customs, and a wide range of divergent histories for its many people who ultimately don't have a common origin. Nigeria will not qualify to be a nation with the common definition of a nation above, but a state only.

There are many other countries all around the world that can only be described as states like Nigeria. According to Pastor Chris Oyakhilome, "A state is ready for prosperity and development when it delivers to its people a robust bill of rights, a sense of liberty, and freedom of expression. The purpose of nations is the realization of human aspirations. It is in pursuance of man's dreams or desires for happiness, prosperity, self-expression, ecological development, self-fulfillment, and its unreachable and unending desire for self-discovery and maximization of intellectual, spiritual, and physical abilities. Since we are humans and cannot attain or achieve all these in isolation but through relationships with like-minded creatures, we must agree to relate together and work together as a state.

"The purpose of states is to form such an association while providing justice, domestic tranquility, and common defense to promote the general welfare and secure their postulated ethnicity for themselves and their posterity. We must remember that every one of us has something to contribute because only Nigerians can help develop Nigeria. All that we require in our nation for our prosperity, security, and progress will come from within us. Therefore, each one of us must be ready and willing to be a vital part of it. It's a very special time in our nation today."

What Africa needs to develop and grow is leadership's sincerity of purpose that can put in place a political system and constitutional framework that would help our country become a thriving state.

In the WaaGovernment book series, the author has given us his inspired ideas; resource material, and academic framework on nation-building patriotism and social change put together in 7 years for the building nation out of the contextualized Nigeria and nationhood in Africa. To achieve a better

country, you must enthrone visionary leadership in
your country.

Towards a Better Country: A quest for visionary
leadership in Africa is a WaaGovernment action
propelling tool on citizenship, democratic
advancement, sustainable development, and
African economic revolution. It is the Series Three
of the Nation Building compendium entitled,
"WaaGovernment and Theory of Nations", a
relationship-inspired work that uses satire and
metaphor in its setting, designed to be acted as a
play on stage.

In the classic work, the inspiring and passionate
words of the author will open the mind, penetrate
the heart and challenge the reader to think big for
his or her country.

This book nurtures love and ignites passion in the heart of the reader to think only to cause a change in his or her country.

The author's target is to build a collaborative spirit in Africans, reactivate national culture, build faith, strengthen trust, raise citizen's conscious awareness for participation, and get them involved in government and governance geared towards achieving visionary leadership that would lead to and speed up progress, peacebuilding, and advanced development in our countries.

The WaaGovernment books series contain the antidote for national challenges in Nigeria. The author has given his heart to this classic work, and he believes that it would be propitious for African schools, governments, and institutions to rebuild the African society in our re-culturing campaigns for a sustained change in the African society, system of leadership and governance that would kill the anti-progress trio of corruption, religion and ethnicity, and many other cultural hindrances responsible for the backwardness of Nigeria and Africa.

I, therefore, implore you to dedicate quality time to reading this classic for an understanding of where we are in the present scheme of things, what has been accomplished, and what is yet to be accomplished. This will enable you to find your place and role on this journey to revamp our country with visionary leadership in our quest for a better country

Ledogo Amabu,

In Towards a Better Country

A quest for visionary leadership in Africa, 2023

Two

TOWARDS A BETTER COUNTRY: THE ROLE OF THE PEOPLE

Nigeria is preparing for the 2023 general election. Owing to the enrichment of our democratic space by virtue of the new electoral act, several Organization and advocacy group campaigning for good governance and effective representation has been inviting me to speak in their programs in our collective desire to see our country working and an economically advanced Africa.

This time, it was "A Youth Arise Campaign" in Port Harcourt and I attend the event with WaaGovernment as a guest speaker.

I was invited on stage and I began my speech with a discussion I had with a friend in the diaspora, Doo-olo-nu Agara who highlighted the salient features of my personality and WaaGovernment's project. He observed and advise, "Hon, as a leader of the people and you must get set for real leadership coaching that would entrench effective leadership in the Nigerian and African system" I felt flattered by my friend's message but was very humbled by his encouragement and genuine concern for our country.

Doo-Olo-nu, who is also addressed by his middle name, Clever, is an Ogoni-born, patriotic Nigerian based in Canada with a background in Engineering and Management. "Do," my young friend always advocates for change, effective representation, and good governance in the system.

It is on the strength of the overwhelming love in my heart and the collective demand of compatriots that I am here today to speak to young electorates and leadership for a change to get our country working and we shall have an inspiring discussion on **"TOWARDS A BETTER THE ROLE OF THE PEOPLE."**

I have emphasized at several fora that during electioneering, in our country, we must support and elect only inspiring and visionary leaders into positions of trust. And am here encouraging you in this youth Rise campaign as the great youth of this great Nation and as leaders of the future to come together and think to build your dear country.

Building a nation requires taking patriotic actions that will protect today and secure the future. If Nigeria can get it right, Africa will get it right!

As Mahatma Gandhi rightly said; "A nation's culture resides in the hearts and the soul of its people". Nigeria has lived without a definite ideology and purpose for a long time, and in this our collective quest and patriotic desire in search of permanent solutions for the decades of prevailing "divisive whirlwind" of national hatred and suspicion with mostly opportunists leaders that have and are occupying the country's political space, I hereby charge you fellow countrymen and women- the young electorates to rise up and press for good governance and quality leadership in your respective constituencies and states. All Nigerian electorates must grow beyond inducement and be bold and courageous in their polling units during elections and stand together as a people against leaders without vision and passion for the people.

In one of my lecture, I made mention of how Political manipulations in the system enables imposition of candidates during electioneering from the party level to the general election itself and how this antidemocratic behavior of despotic leaders has deprived Nigeria and Nigerians of quality leadership and, our constituencies' effective representation. It is the bane of Nigeria's leadership failure and the reason for underdevelopment and a major cause of insecurity and poverty in our country today. The corrupt system has produced more leaders who neither love the country nor their people and those who do not think about the collective growth and progress of the people in the long term.

The purpose of government at all levels of governance is to provide security, and social amenities, and build enabling business environment and opportunities for the people in every community in the federation. This has been lacking in Nigeria the giant of Africa. Our country must get it right to lead the struggle to restore the pride of Africa among the comity of nations.

As citizens, we must see the country as our own community and think to become drivers of change. To build our country, we must have passion for our country. Passion for our country is the elixir needed for real development, sustainable progress, and peacebuilding in Nigeria. As young people, we must all believe in the unity and victory of our country as we support only inspiring, experienced, and patriotic leaders with vision in the general elections.

Nigeria is a great country that's divinely blessed with abundant material and Human Resources, yet unable to realize its full potential and fulfillment of purpose due to leadership failure and successive unstable systems which subsequently resulted in unbelievable, reckless, and systematic corruption.

To change the narrative and to redefine the future, we must go for leaders who have the people at heart at all levels of government; all those seeking our votes at the state house, House of Representatives, Senate, Governorship, and the Big one, the Presidency of the federal republic of Nigeria should be scaled on the balance of their past records, pedigree, and contributions to nation building and in community service

It's been said that the problem of Nigeria is not about a particular president or government in power but the absence of a working system that will enhance productivity and strengthen the people's faith in their country.

Those who hold such an opinion cannot be disproved because it is only Nigerians that can help develop Nigeria. "All that is required for our progress, our prosperity, and security will come from within us; we are the ones to do it," Pastor Chris Oyakhilome said,

Nigeria's challenge is a foundational problem and as such, we must impress on those seeking our votes on their plans and agenda for true federalism and having a true people's constitution for a solid foundation of development and peace in Nigeria. To advance the country in peace, unity, and development, we must set aside all ethnic and religious considerations and come together to reconstruct our own country. We must invest in the limitless, untapped, and abundant resources spread across the length and breadth of a country blessed beyond oil.

At the state level, Leadership must be compelled by a vision and not just the provision of physical infrastructure but we must equally take all necessary actions and create a new system and environment that impacts the thinking process and the productivity of our people. Government without politics must always support our youths to aspire and to win in business, career, and private ventures. Government is for the people; there must be a genuine effort to invest in the young population and the girl child.

Leaders can't have their own kids in foreign universities but see educational policies that provide scholarships and educational incentives to citizens as a waste of resources. Nigeria's educational system should be developed to an internationally acceptable standard. We need compassionate leaders, those who connect with the people.

We need visionary leadership in our states. Being a governor of a state is a serious business and as such, political parties should sponsor only prepared, experienced candidates and those who have built visible working systems.

To get it right, and for sustainable change, the electorates must rise up, reject money bags in the system and resist manipulative tendencies and all unpatriotic wild instincts working towards imposing uninspired loyalists and subjects on the people and into government for selfish purposes.

Nigerian voters of all divides, creeds and languages must go into the electioneering process with eyes wide open. You must ask questions about Citizens' welfare, education, health, human capital development, and above all, the readiness of would-be leaders in the commitment to supporting a functional federal and secular country where nepotism in government should end and a country where religion should be left in the hands of free choice.

Three

THE QUEST FOR OF VISIONARY LEADERSHIP IN AFRICA

It was the Niger Delta-born philanthropist and business tycoon, Chief Barr. Dumo Lulu Briggs, who while talking to his kinsmen in his Nigerian country home, Abonnema, said,

"Leadership must be about the collective good; peace and progress in the society. So, while it may be necessary to seek thrones and power, people must truly give priority to the need of the people for social harmony and development I believe that anyone with this mindset will not seek power at the expense of communal love".

What we need in Africa today is dynamic, inspiring, patriotic, and courageous leaders to govern the country for the good of all and the next generation.

And as Pastor Sam Adeyemi, an elder statesman and a patriot, opined: *"the older generation needs to think ahead about our legacy. Africans have suffered a lot throughout history. We have a duty to rise above prejudices and selfishness to create an environment where potentials can flourish, and where leadership is accountable and poised for service"*.

"Indeed, there is a future for our country but there is also a compelling need for a sustainable campaign for Change through visionary leadership to make the next generation believe trust, and love their country, exploring the boundless opportunities and her beautiful and richly endowed resources."

Visionary leadership is a challenge in Africa. We need knowledgeable and patriotic leaders who love the country and are compassionate about the well-being of the people. We need leaders trained to think ahead and drive growth and development to the continent. We need leaders who can lead to lift our countries to greater heights and mobilize the people to take action for the building of Africa.

The possibility of Africa being on the world decision-making table in the future is collectively resolved and our patriotic support for only inspiring and visionary leadership to lead in the Government.

There are over 1.3 billion people in Africa and millions of Africans in the Diaspora. We live in the second-biggest continent by landmass and the wealthiest continent in terms of human and natural resources. By these indices, Africa as a continent is expected to play a lead role in the world decision-making table, but we have been lagging for decades because of a lack of visionary leadership. Africans must come together to change the narrative and create our own stories.

The future of Africa is in the hands of the trained and inspired students of nation-building and those who live in their country and not the uninspired and selfish leaders waiting for hope in the hands of kind white foreigners. We must know that only Africans can make Africa Great!

In the past, we have had those who dare for a change but were betrayed and marked for elimination like Thomas Sankara of Burkina Faso among many others, who wanted to correct the negative impact of Neo-Colonialism and post-independence imperialism in Africa. But time has passed any nation that desires advancement can actually grow with visionary leadership and patriotic citizens who are united.

With visionary leadership and unity of purpose, our countries will grow and advance. We must build and strengthen our regional and continental relationships and enter only working -reliable multi-lateral partnerships. We are aware, no nation can do it alone, we need interdependence, interrelationships, regional collaboration, and continental ties to sustain and advance peaceful co-existence."

I ended my speech and with rousing applause, I was ushered off the stage.

The award session began and I was invited upstage as an awardee. Upon receiving the award, I dedicated it to WaaGovernment for her inspiring

personality and support in Nation Building and I
beckoned on her to join me on stage.

With a shy smile on her face, she embraced me
and the microphone was given to her to say
something. And a very short one,
WaaGovernment just greeted the young audience
and turn to me "thank you so greatly sir for your
passionate love for our country and your
dedication in passing the message of change I love
you" while WaaGovernment was talking to me on
stage,   the young audience gaze at us with
admiration. It was a beautiful scene and an
inspiring moment.   WaaGovernment has been
indeed a great partner in nation-building.

Four

KNOWLEDGE AND ACTION FOR BUILDING AFRICA

I was developing a lecture on what African leaders must know and the actions we must take to build Africa and in the course of the work, I read and had a series of meditations that tremendously increased my understanding of topical issues about Africa and her development. One beautiful weekend, I invited WaaGovernment to tell her a story about what happened to Africa in the past and what we need now to move forward. She came and while we discussed, I made her comfortable with so many beautiful stories about leadership and African history with respect to development. She listened to me and was so inspired.

Join WaaGovernment to participate in our home class lecture as I explain more:

"Historically, Africans were never slaves to any nation. Africa is a land blessed by God with so many abundant natural resources, and a home to people of resilient spirit. But in a certain era, countries with more organized leadership came and conquered nations in Africa. The resources of Africa were forcefully and selfishly taken away to build Europe and the West. Europe and the west should hide their face in shame for hypocritically seeking to repatriate stolen artifacts from Africa when what is needed by them is the handoff of decades of parasitic influence and unhealthy tendencies as seen in Francophone countries where

France is still sucking those sovereign African nations dry.

And at this point in the history of Africa, what Nigeria needs is a genuine design and support for the functionality of her peculiar system and a working people's constitution that genuinely provides liberty, freedom, equity, and justice to every Nigerian citizen. All evil and parasitic colonial impediments and negative political, social & economic influences must be set aside to allow Nigeria to build a competitive-productive economy. Nigeria is the giant of Africa. She must stand up, grow and advance for the realization of her potential and the prosperity of her people. She must respect her diversity and decentralize power to reflect that diversity and enhance productivity and end corruption in the system. She must create a working system where every Nigerian can grow, aspire and win. If Nigeria can get it right, Africa will get it right!

Africa has moved and is moving forward, thus Europe and Britain must specifically apologize and pay reparation for the sin committed Against Africa, not the deceptive restoration of stolen artifacts. As a patriot and a change companion, seeking solutions to the development and nationhood challenges facing Africa, I am calling on African sovereign states to be watchful against Chinese-coded business languages in bilateral and multilateral trade agreements and misleading advice from global bodies masquerading as protection of African interest. This is similar to what was witnessed in the social adjustment program during the Babangida regime by the World Bank and International Monitory Fund (IMF) among many selfish globalists induced policies to keep Africa under.

Africans must self-examine and look internally to dump any value and system that has made our nations underdeveloped and unproductive. Our people were made to believe in the superiority of the white in Europe and America but Civilisation and education have proven wrong the fallacy of inequality in the Human DNA, with the exploits of Africans the world over, it is now a fact that there is no superior mental intelligence of the Caucasians- the Europeans, the Americans, the Chinese, the Russians, the Indians, the Arabs and even the Jews and many other nations created by God. The developed nations, all achieved development through the power of ideas, patriotism, and visionary leadership. So the building of a nation starts at the midpoint of visionary leadership, knowledge (education), and unity of purpose of the people.

We have seen Singapore, China, and UAE-Dubai move from very poor nations in a very short time in history to becoming powerful economies and technological giants in the world. This is possible because of visionary leadership who mobilized the people and made them see and think for their country. When you have leaders that think to produce and government with the willpower to deploy the country's commonwealth and resources for the building of their nation, no force from the pit of hell can stop the growth and development of such countries.

All that is needed to birth a productive economy in Africa is visionary leadership and unity of purpose. So, at the moment, any nation can develop and grow into nationhood no matter the experience of the past. Africa needs visionary leadership. She needs leaders full of passion, dedication, patriotism, zeal, and selflessness to serve and lead our countries.

With visionary leadership, we can stand as a people and birth a new system in our countries. Most African countries are practicing democracy, which is good because the people should be responsible for who governs them. Our votes during the electioneering process are what can do the magic in our quest for credible and visionary leadership to build Africa. We must take action to elect visionary and credible leaders by the use of our franchise-our voting power. We must all get involved in the process to rebuild our country.

Social consciousness is key to building our country. You must take interest in your national affairs. You must know your immediate environment. You must ask the right questions to get the right answers from your leaders as a conviction of your support. You must learn to be engaged in the conversation of power and leadership. You must know how our budgets work. You must know who will lead you before party primaries. Political parties must have clear-cut objectives and philosophies. We must be interested in who represents us and who is being presented to run elections on the mandate of political parties.

As GEORGE ORWELL said, "People Who Elect Corrupt Politicians, Impostors, Thieves, and Traitors are not Victims...But Accomplices." We must know that nothing would change unless we take action, be interested, get involved, and ask the right questions. The people cannot choose to be accomplices and expect a change. We must always choose to stand for something. We must decide to support and elect leaders with vision and passion for our country. Passion for our country is the

antidote and solution for Africa's nationhood
challenges.

Change in the scheme of things in Africa requires
citizens' unity of purpose and massive participation
of visionary men and women in politics, and you
reading this the hope and future of Africa. You
have been inspired and trained to cause a change.
Right there where you are, in your community and
sphere of contact, you must stand for what is right
and know when you do, you are standing for your
country. Amongst peers, in your street and all your
undertakings, become a leader to be rallied around
and reckoned with. Always choose to speak for
your country by stepping out and taking up the
responsibility to advance the progress of your
community. By doing so, you are standing for your
country. You must decide to always stand by only
visionary and inspiring selfless leaders who have
what it takes to represent you and your people in

government. You must stand for the right course. Your decision to stand out and be the change you desire in your country is the best decision you could ever take. Do things and be reassured of a permanent place in the good book of history and posterity. You must remember, you are the change you desire for your country. Things must change and, there must be a landmark for change."

I ended my story and WaaGovernment asked me "sir what is expected from citizens and Africans in learning from the past and to effect a real change in the scheme of things?

I responded, "We cannot change our history but we can do something about the future. We can decide and redirect our collective conscious efforts to change the events of today to redefine our tomorrow with our actions today. When you Join or support the "Africa Re-cultured Campaign" and the "Love for Country Campaign" by the WaaGovernment Consult for Winsome Africa Agenda, you are actually supporting a citizen's movement and a patriotic cause aimed at training, inspiring, and raising visionary leaders to build Africa and those to provide answers to nationhood questions in your country"

She shouted Wow! But there is a compelling need for nationhood in Nigeria considering her diverse nature and internal division retrogressively working against the growth of our country. I said yes, Nigeria needs to unite or decide on her future above internal crises. I then bring out a paper I have developed on Quest for Nationhood.

Five

THE QUEST FOR NATIONHOOD IN NIGERIA

In an article titled ''Shonekan and a country in search of a Sage,'' I read in one of Nigeria's national dailies. The author writes,

"Since independence, in 1960, many problems have rocked Nigeria to its foundations ruining the promise of a country which once held the priceless promise of becoming Africa's first world superpower. From the first military coup in 1966, which precipitated a calamitous and precipitous civil war in 1967, to subsequent military coups, military regimes of dubious legacies, and Nigeria's struggles to enshrine accountable democracy since 1999.

The giant of Africa has known rapid depreciation in the hands of those who would falter a giant"

After I read the above article on the search for a sage in Nigeria, I was moved and began to think, why despite population advantage and our beautiful diversity, growth is distorted in a promising country, I then understood that the major cause of instability and the reasons for the trend is because we have not been able to make considerable effort and patriotic attempts to come together and build the fragile country handed over to our founding fathers by the British in our collective desire and quest for Nationhood in Nigeria.

Nationhood is the building of a country to think and stay together with pride. In Nigeria's past leaders and successive governments pursued nationalism instead of nationhood. It is the course of NIGERIA backwardness and stunted growth since independence.

"A Nation is a large number of people organized under a body of government and sharing common customs, origin, history or language'. But such a definition cannot go for a country like NIGERIA that has different languages, diverse customs, and a wide range of divergent histories for its many peoples who ultimately don't have a common origin. Nigeria will not qualify to be a nation with the common definition of a nation above, but a state only. There are many other countries all around the world that can only be described as states like Nigeria. According to Pastor Chris Oyakhilome, "A state is ready for prosperity and development when it delivers to its people a robust bill of rights, a sense of liberty, and freedom of expression. The purpose of nations is the realization of human aspirations, it is in pursuance of man's dreams or desires for happiness, prosperity, self-expression ecological development, self-fulfillment, and unreachable and unending desire for self-discovery and maximization of intellectual, Spiritual, and physical abilities. Since we are humans and cannot attain or achieve all these in isolation, but through relationships with like-minded creatures, we must agree to relate together and work together as a state. "The purpose of states is to form such association providing justice, domestic tranquility, and common defense, promote the general welfare and secure their postulated ethnicity for themselves and their posterity, we must remember that every one of us has something to give, something to contribute because only Nigerians can help develop Nigeria. All that we require in our nation for our prosperity, our security, and our progress will come from within us. Therefore, each one of us must be ready and willing to be a vital part of it. It's a very special time in our nation today."

What Africa needs to develop and grow is leadership and sincerity of purpose to put in place a political system and constitutional framework that will help our country become a thriving state. "Thriving States are those who, through education and culture, have helped their people develop into nationhood," the man of God said.

Nigeria is a beautiful country believed by patriots to have been born of the divine idea. A residence of people of resilient spirit and a country replete with a full load of human and natural resources, but for a long time, Nigeria has been fulfilling scripts handed to her by those who cannot love her or desire her stability and real progress more than

their own people and country. It is the reason
Britain and the West were forever silent on
Nigeria's non-functionality of the nation's
refineries and the country's politics of oil, the
destruction of the Nigerian environment, ecology,
and heritage.

That we have blindly pursued the wrong purpose
for our country since independence calls for
courageous and visionary leadership for sustained
change.

I have stated, severally, that only visionary
leadership and unity of purpose can make us
achieve our dream of Nationhood.

In the nation-building article in chapter one I read
for WaaGovernment, I declared,

"No Nation Can progress without a common
vision and a common purpose."

It is a pity Nigeria has existed for a long time without a defined purpose and vision as a country!

We cannot continue to pursue a wrong purpose and a system designed to fail and expect to progress. "No country that is programmed to administrate and not to produce can prosper."

Since the return of civilian rule in 1999, Nigeria runs a constitutional democracy. The various states are the countries federating units as enshrined in our constitution, but the issues at stake to be addressed for the country to develop and grow into nationhood are the concerns and the consequences of the loud natures of the various distinct ethnic groups singing ethnic solidarity songs for self-existence because of perceived injustice in the land.

In our quest for nationhood for our beloved country, the various ethnic nationality or micronations in Nigeria must resolve to live together as one while the government must accept that sustaining a unitary system in Nigeria is evil and against the spirit of federalism. We must constitutionally put in place systems that support our collective survival while at all times, patriotically encouraging our people to accept Nigeria's diversity as we embrace the reality of our diversity by coming together to enact a "People's Constitution" that will end the cry of injustice in Nigeria and consolidate peacebuilding and national unity to keep Nigeria the pride of Africa since independence and at the return to civilian rule 1919, many ethnic nationalities in the federation have been showing more loyalty to their blood and ethnic roots than continued allegiance to the country. This cannot continue in our quest for nationhood.

Successive leadership has failed to provide solutions to the plethora of challenges confronting Nigeria as a Nation. There has been so much agitation for secession. To get this checked and stopped, we must accept, choose and elect leaders who can think and those with the vision to transform the country and lift the people's hope and aspirations.

"Nations are not built through loyalty to blood, culture, and geographical location but through the pursuit of a common purpose." What Nigeria needs is inspiring visionary and patriotic leadership to build our country to realize her dream as a nation and our progress as a people.

A nation's culture resides in the hearts and the soul of its people. Our country needs to discover and pursue its purpose as a nation.

Until the purpose of a country is discovered, the driving forces behind the policies and decisions of the Government will still be largely negatively influenced by ethnocentric forces, greed, and personal pursuits backed by external centrifugal forces working against the general progress of Sub-Saharan Africa and Nigeria in particular.

A country whose people are walking parallel cannot succeed. For a country to experience a change, Leadership and the people's love for their country must be directly proportional. For things to change, the love for the various countries that makes up Africa must be strong enough to outshine ethnic enclaves.

For "One Nigeria" to work, Nigerians must come together and agree to chart a new course.

We have lived without unity of purpose. We must not be afraid to engage in political reconstruction and discussion that would make Nigeria prosper.

Nigeria will prosper more in a fairly decentralized system with a competitive regional economy than in a centralized system only working for the families of the elites and their foreign parasitic allies.

For peacebuilding, trust, and an indivisible Nigeria, we must do away with all forms of systematic injustice and nepotism and put in practice, a structural framework that balance and support the stability of our nations through the provision of equal opportunities and freedom for the People.

When a people come together with one intention to build their own country and pursue a common purpose, all other challenges facing their country and the people will surrender to the decisions of unity of purpose.

Government exists for the people. We must look inward and address the concerns and genuine complaints to strengthen the trust and confidence of the people of the Federal Republic of Nigeria.

Nigeria needs visionary and purpose-driven leadership with the required competency in all strata of government and governance. Politics should not be left in the hands of politicians alone. Patriots must step in and mobilize the people for a change.

During electioneering, we must resolve to support only proven and tested- visionary leaders with uncommon courage and patriotism in government to move the country forward. The people should always come together, think, and decide beyond political sentiments, region, and religion. This would be achieved by a high literacy rate and the entrenchment of democratic institutions as it was in India.

When this is done poverty, unemployment, and illiteracy, the root cause of insecurity in our country will be history.

We need leaders with passion and the capacity to mobilize our countrymen and women for success and prosperity. No kind foreigner will build our country for us. You are the change we need for a better country.

Nigeria is too blessed to be poor. The growth of a country is directly proportional to the vision and inspiration of leadership. We need a government that will support universities to become real research societies and centers for solutions to the country's challenges. We need a value-added system; we need a government that can create an enabling environment for businesses to drive. We need a private sector-driven economy.

Our Institutions must become stronger than the dictates of the whims and caprices of individuals. Our electioneering processes and systems must be completely free from certain political cabal's control. The Judicial and legislative arms of government must be supported and allowed to be independent. The Local Government too should be completely autonomous.

The people, on the other hand, must stand for the country in patriotism to support security agencies in the defense of our country and sovereignty. The military and security architecture must be supported and encouraged to steer clear from politics but service for the nation's respect for democratic authorities.

We must all work together and put in place stronger systems that can birth sustainable, inspiring, patriotic, and visionary leadership to help the country fulfill its purpose and achieve greatness as a people.

To end this paper, I will borrow the notable words of the famous Abraham Lincoln of the USA that said "The best way to predict your future is to create it."

Nigeria in particular and Africa in general must learn to practice democracy in line with our local realities for sustainable development to be achieved.

Six

BUILDING THE ECONOMIC MUSCLES OF AFRICA

WaaGovernment met Dr. Jewel Oghene, an Afrocentric lecturer in Economics & Geopolitics, from the Ken Saro Wiwa University- Zoro East-West road, Ogoniland, During a lecture on indigenous resource utilization and management at the 25th Ken Saro Wiwa Memorial Lecture on the Campus.

Through WaaGovernment, I became close to Dr. Jewel Oghene and in one of our discussions, we touched on salient issues affecting Nigeria's production capacity and the negative impact of

Africa's over-consumption of foreign products. She explained to me the Geopolitics of oil and the need for Nigeria to elect patriotic leaders who have knowledge of how the economy runs. This is for an earnest rebuilding of Nigeria's economy through the promotion of indigenous products.

She also recommended to me a book entitled, "The Black Swan" by Teleb, a vastly entertaining writer with a polymathic command of subjects ranging from Cognitive Science to Business to Probability Theory that would not only expand one's knowledge but would definitely change one's perspective about the world.

The reason for most wars in the world is resource-based. Europe and the West have been spent; they are running out of funds and innovative means of making money. After utilizing Africa's natural energy resources in the processes of industrialization, they turned against resource-rich states demanding they stop the production of oil.

Green and Earth-friendly campaigners/activists from Africa are sincerely ignorant, working for Western interests, advising Africa to keep her oil in the ground to deprive us of the utilization of our rich resources in our developmental activities. This is to keep Africa dependent on their emerging "Eco-friendly market."

For instance, Nigeria has billions of barrels of crude oil yet to be utilized and has signed agreements not to use them, but rather, to utilize eco-friendly energy sources. The industrial sector which will help produce these types of machinery is still lagging compared to its competitors and fellow signatories.

In the Energy sector, our refineries have been shut down and a nation rich in natural gas and oil is still scrambling to stand tall. It is therefore wise that Nigerians be wary of the sustained effort for the removal of subsidies which is engineered by external parties.

This knowledge is encapsulated in the concept of the Geopolitics of oil. It is the new colonial game plan of the West designed to keep Africa and developing nations like Nigeria dependent on them.

China, India, Israel, and even Japan started the move for the promotion of indigenous products. With the development of their manufacturing sector, these nations' economies grew exponentially.

Drawing from the experience of the above nations, their game plan was to keep Africa, especially Nigeria, under. To destroy Africa's industrial reputation as she is being bombarded with imported goods. The target is to crumble the industrial capacity of our nations. Thus, the term "Aba made" or "Nigeria made" became a tool for the destruction of the morale of our manufacturing sector. The trust in foreign-made products was fostered and within 10 years the level of consumerism in Nigeria increased by over 100%. Importation classes became the mainstay and the dumping of foreign goods on us increased.

The backward and forward linkage advantage gotten over time was eroded as local firms could no longer compete with the foreign cheap products, hence crumbling the industrial capacity of the nation.

As a holder of a B.Tech in Geology and Mining, having a special interest in economic geology, I know how rich Nigeria is. From the sedimentary basin in Southern Nigeria, with deposits of Ajale sandstone for construction and kaolinite clay for pharmaceutical companies, paint productions, ceramics, and detergent as well as Shale deposits for hydrocarbon trap that can also be used for drugs, hydrocarbon in its full crude content—to the basement complex in the Western and Northern Nigeria with Gold, Diamond, Marbles for tiles, granite for construction, Lithium for electrical battery production with its rich deposit in Taraba, Jos, and other Northern states are among the over 250 economic minerals in Nigeria.

Every state in Nigeria is blessed with economic minerals that can turn the economy around. And she has no business with poverty in the eyes of nature and man. The challenge with Nigeria has been leadership. In electing new leaders, we must think to get it right to rebuild our economic Muscles.

We need patriotic leaders equipped with the knowledge to build our country, grow our Gross Domestic Product (GDP), and enhanced our export goods base. Nigeria must build her per capita income to lift her people out of poverty. Africa cannot keep producing opportunists and ill-informed leaders whose only interest in government is to siphon the people's common resources for their personal aggrandizement and expect to grow and develop. Success is not accidental, it is a conscious effort put together over time to produce the desired outcome and outputs.

Nigerians should look out for patriotic leaders who will "work the talk" and those to promote our indigenous products because until this is achieved like in the 80s when 1 dollar was equivalent to 70 kobos, Nigeria's forex crises and high cost of living will not end and our economy will not grow."

Nigerian leaders must as a matter of urgency think to convert her young population and human resources to oil wells in every state in the federation in our collective desire to build our economy. Like Dr. Joseph Obele, a Business Development and entrepreneurship expert and a Lecturer with Ken Saro Wiwa Polytechnic Bori rightly posited "Human capital development is the only instrument for Nation building. Entrepreneurship development is the biggest weapon to fight insecurity."

This should also be a major direction for Nigeria in our patriotic quest to rebuild our economic powers.

At this phase in African history, we must forget western unpatriotic advice and think to build our land. Nigeria needs Patriotic and decisive leaders to build her economic muscles.

Africans must embrace local production and indigenous products and services. Nigeria's economic minerals and our rich energy source must be harnessed and used for the development and revitalization of Nigeria's economy. Our vast land which is good for agriculture and tourism must be used to revive the economy of Nigeria. The giant of Africa must rise above external deception and internal contradictions and unite to rebuild her economy and our country. This is the way nations are built.

Towards a Better country in Africa, there is a compelling need for visionary patriotic leadership for the good of the people and the rebuilding of Nigeria. And because Nigeria and most African countries have chosen to practice democracy, the next phase of our discussion will x-ray democracy in view of our local realities for sustainable development in Africa.

Seven

DEMOCRACY AND SUSTAINABLE DEVELOPMENT IN AFRICA

I joined WaaGovernment to meet Dr. Bunmi in her office. She happens to be WaaGovernment's mentor and our leader in the church. Dr. Bunmi is a virtuous woman, an influencer, and a model to many young people.

She offered us seats and was extremely delighted to see us and expressed complete satisfaction as she applauded and encouraged us to take our beautiful friendship to the next level. While we were still listening, Dr. Bunmi looked at WaaGovernment in the face, then turn to me and gave us a kind smile, telling us our motivating relationship is endorsed.

Dr. Continued, "I was told both of you have been attending programs together motivating young people to love and to believe in their country, and to be agents of Change."

I responded, "Yes, Dr. Ma."

She then requested that I should be part of the topical guest on the expansion of democracy and sustainable development in Africa that would be shared at a conference she was organizing. I was truly overwhelmed with the opportunity and privilege of being part of her event. WaaGovernment then told Dr. Bunmi to inform the leadership of her organization to expect the best of moments because she trusts what I can do.

Our meeting with Dr. Bunmi ended, and we booked a *bolt* ride to Genesis Cinema in GRA Port

Harcourt for an evening date, and to watch a movie together.

On the day of the event, WaaGovernment and I were seated, waiting patiently for the program to commence. I was then invited to speak, and after all protocols were observed, I began to speak!

"Change happens at the resolve of citizens of goodwill, and at the arrival of men and women of courage and vision.

"History has shown us and other nations that since the cradle of civilization, many nations have evolved and gone through different phases of growth and development. Many have built strong institutions like the USA, above the whims and caprice of individuals and leaders. While many had grown, developed, and made their country great and a better place to live, many other countries too have emerged and grown, and are experiencing record change and tremendous development to become modern civilized societies in a short period like the Asian giants. But many in Africa are still struggling to start the race and their hope is in time because most great countries you see today were yesterday, not better than Africa. They develop and grow not by the color of their skin but by the power of vision in leadership, love for country, and unity of purpose - the agenda and purpose we are gathered here today for us to be informed and be inspired to start thinking as a people.

Americans and many other nations can today choose the kind of leadership they want and desire by themselves, but yesterday women and people of color, Africans, and other natives weren't allowed to vote talk less leading the country. We witnessed improvement and changes in the American system over time. We have seen Obama, an African -

American and many other examples that had emerged by the power of the ballot and free choice of the people for the victory of democracy. This and many more examples in several countries' development indices have anchored our hope and faith in our awareness campaign to advance our nascent democracy, and to establish sustainable development in the system.

Nations like India among many others have evolved and have experienced rapid changes in a short time because of investment in education and entrenchment of democratic values and institutions. And I can tell you, there is also hope for Nigeria and Africa if we can only learn from India.

Many nations have achieved organized systems where citizens' rights are been promoted and protected. When the people's votes count and visionary leadership is allowed to emerge, nations grow and develop very fast like in the case of India where medical tourism is number one in the world. This is what unity of purpose, patriotism, love, and vision can achieve in a short time in Nigeria and Africa.

In light of the above, we must rise up for our country. We must step out and refuse to be spectators but players for change in the system. We must stand in support of credible and visionary leadership at all levels. We must focus on visionary leadership in the system and keep building faith in our country.

To build Nigeria, the giant of Africa, there is a dire need for collective and individual patriotic actions.

Patriotism is a potent force for the achievement of nationhood and a key factor to unlock the doors of sustainable development and to consolidate democratic values. This is the reason we must sustain reforms that allow a free system where human rights are protected and citizens' lives are justly secured.

We are here on a Reformation Campaign - a campaign for a change in our National culture. Change in our nation is what we aim at achieving and we must teach our young generation to stand as one people and confront the hydra-headed monsters and anti-nation triplet of corruption, ethnicity, and religion - the 3 deadly brothers selfishly used by enemies to destroy the fabric of unity, progress, and development in our country.

Africa is a continent with the highest number of the younger population and we must at all times support the consolidation of democratic values on the continent to avoid the recurrence of the Arab Spring that swept across Northern Africa in the early 21 Century. The youth don't need to destroy their country to vent their frustration and anger on the ruling elite but as young persons, you can speak out and consciously mobilize the people to make the government accountable and vote for better leaders and have those with a visible vision to lead in your country.

"Democracy is a government of the people, by the people and for the people" as defined by Abraham Lincoln, and as such, citizens must be aware of the power of their votes in the achievement of visionary leadership and for the building of a new Africa. Also, African nation-states must know that working together to open up Africa will encourage and strengthen economic growth and regional prosperity.

In Nigeria, restructuring the system and the birth of a new constitution fashioned after the 1963 constitution with few exceptions on the role of the Queen of England in Nigeria's sovereignty will not only open up the system but enhance effective leadership and the practice of true federalism which would help curb corruption and insecurity.

We must open up the system for patriotic, younger, brighter minds to contribute because the growth and success of Nigeria need brave and fair-minded leaders with the political will to implement policies that will drive our system above ethno-religious sentiments. Men of goodwill and patriots in the diaspora must come in to participate and contribute to the building of their beloved country and Africa.

Developed nations were built by men and women of vision with knowledge. Politics is too important to be left in the hands of selfish politicians alone. For a change, Patriots and men of vision must step in and actively participate in the process and be involved in their country's democratic process and governance to help consolidate African nascent democracy because citizens' actions and participation in politics will bring about dynamic leadership and good governance in the system.

To enhance democracy in Africa and to open up the system of Nigeria, we must support the girl child in Northern Nigeria and expose our women to quality education. The female gender must be empowered to grow above all cultural hindrances and stigmatization. They must be educationally equipped to be free and bold to compete and win among male folks by actively getting involved in the process to take charge of the powerhouse of the nation and to occupy not only the other rooms but in the engine rooms of development and Nation building in Africa.

African women must stand up and get involved in leadership. Women are expected to use their intellectual power and influence to effect positive and developmental changes that will bring about good governance like the Late Prof. Dora Akunyili of the then NAFDAC, Chimamanda Adichie - our African literary star that used the power of literature and her various works of art to protect and advance Nigeria and Africa at large. Like these examples, African women must refuse to be limited.

I have repeatedly said in my various lectures and I am here without prejudice to other nations that Africa is a blessed land, but her challenge has been leadership. Most past African leaders came into power on the continent as good men but turned into despots and tyrants. They became demigods in their countries and states by working against their own people because of greed and the ill quest for materialism.

When you sell your soul and corrupt your spirit with greed, you will become wicked and serve only your ego while in power. Such leaders must remember that gaining the whole world and losing their own souls is gaining nothing, and posterity will remember them as a villain and a coward who under-developed their own country and made their own people poor. You will be remembered as the man or woman who failed your country and Africa.

What a shame we must all avoid in our generation!

It is a shame that most African leaders collaborated with external parasitic forces to deprive their people of a good living. They stock African valued assets and resources in the West, in Europe, and in

America for decades, and left Africa and her people empty and poor.

Most African leaders travel to other civilized and developed countries but refuse the ray of visionary leadership that shines in the street of those countries to brighten their thoughts. In wickedness, our leaders for decades refused the beam of Patriotism that transformed the developed world not to penetrate their minds.

This is so sad. It is now time for Nigerians to come together to redesign and reconstruct the Nigerian system for leaders to see public offices as an opportunity to serve and not to loot.

If Dubai, an arid desert can be built by the power of visionary leadership to become the tourist center of the world, why can't the Niger Delta! The region is still underdeveloped after trillions of naira were released for the development of the region by the

Federal government and development partners. This is sad!

Niger Delta leaders must be challenged by the Dubai example.

The book "MY VISION" BY MUHAMMED IBN KALID, THE EMIR OF DUBAI, gives more details on how UAE does not have rivers and seas. It's an arid desert land but guess what? The Government created artificial lakes all of which look like normal rivers. You won't know until you are told.

Nigeria with an increasing population, resources, and human capacity development potential is yet to be developed because of failed leadership and corruption.

Corruption can only be curbed when we have more patriots in power to build the New Nigeria of our dream.

Patriotism makes honest and sincere leadership possible. Accountability and zero tolerance for corruption have made an arid desert land produce springs of lakes in UAE.

The emergence of a country like UAE, Indonesia, Malaysia, and other emerging Asian regional economic blocs has made any seeming excuse by Nigerian and African leaders a lame one.

Nigeria's greatness is not only in our decision to stay together but our collective resolve to support only visionary leadership in our states and countries to advance democracy and sustain development in the country.

It is believed to be expensive and should be discarded but if Nigeria has decided to adopt the same kind of government (democracy) as the United States of America, then she must equally go for what works for the most popular developed democracy in the world while we take into account our local realities to advance and to succeed.

Passion for our country is the panacea needed to build Nigeria. Americans were able to do it because of extreme patriotism.

Patriotism is an act of love, and love is an eternal value. God is love, so the God embraced in Nigeria and Africa should be used to make a change in the scheme of things as it was in America and many European nations. There must be a change in the national culture of Nigeria to end the corruption destroying a great country put together by God, though many call Nigeria a mistake by the British. I don't think so but we should recreate and sustain the system where the gospel plays a vital role in the African Reformation process as advised by the author of God's General, Dr. Robert Liardon, in his visit to the Dunamis Rain of Revival Conference in 2021 in Abuja.

The United States of America became powerful because it was founded on freedom and justice. The freedom enjoyed in America was made possible by the vision statements of the American founding fathers. The Constitution of the USA produces strong institutions, not strong men. In any country where leadership revolves around only a few elites, opportunities will not abound but greed-induced poverty.

Lack of patriotism is the cause of greed responsible for decades of discontent, distrust, wickedness, and sustained crises in Nigeria - a land blessed by God with enormous human and natural resources.

Nigeria must be allowed to remain a circular state. Religious bigots must be watched. What Nigeria needs are leaders who love the country to advance, develop and prosper her.

Love is a force for change. The light of true love comes from God. Citizens must "arise and shine", and get involved in politics. We must be interested in the governance of our country and the government of our states for "one of the penalties for refusing to participate in politics is that you end up being governed by your inferiors" - PLATO

"The wise who refuse to rule should prepare to suffer the rule of idiots" - Socrates.

The change our country needs to grow and develop would come from you the patriot listening to me, and those of you who have read my books - The WaaGovernment Book series written and designed to train and inspire young people and transit generation to love their country and to build their nation. This is a product of The WaaGovernment for Winsome African Agenda, an organization whose goals and objectives aim at the institutionalization of innovative leadership in governance and to instill purposefulness amongst the youths and transit generation across Africa. Poised to reawaken the African communal spirit and to turn African adversities into amazing advantages in our quest to preserve a productive and persevering posterity for the crystallization of a culture of Excellence, we are building and molding students of nation-building to take charge of their country, to rise, mobilize and galvanize the people to use the power of the ballot to get their country working.

Living is for everyone but leadership is not for everyone.

Brave visionary citizenry who have seen the light and have been inspired must step in and participate in the politics of the nations for a change.

We must train and teach our children to stand for their country and to act as patriots. Our wards must be taught in schools how to be passionate about their country and to be agents of change. We must influence their thinking process at a young age to reject bribery and inducement, and to build in them integrity for the desired change in their country. These are values they must grow up with.

The identity of the greatness of the country must be written in their hearts and their minds. We must culture our people on how to decide and choose only visionary and purpose-driven men and women of ideas for leadership positions for a change in our nations.

Africa needs visionary leaders.

We need leaders who can think for Africa to open her up for regional prosperity through the power of unity and bigger markets that can change the African economy".

I ended my lecture and there were thunderous claps of applause and standing ovations.

Amidst the shouts, I could see WaaGovernment beaming her impressive face and mild smile at me. She stood up and walked up to me on the stage and gave me a big hug in the presence of the audience as we stepped outside.

The event ended, and Dr. Bunmi later joined us and took us out to buy WaaGovernment some gifts as she was expected to return back to Bauchi for a pass out from her national youths' service the next week.

Eight

CONCLUSION

JOIN US TO TAKE ACTION TO BUILD OUR COUNTRY

A visionary and passionate kind of leadership is what we need to produce a working and productive country. Leadership is everything to sustainable development and the rebuilding of a country. And I concurred with Mr. Peter Obi when he stated during his 2023 presidential campaign tour to Nigerians in the diaspora in Toronto Canada, that, "We will emphasize patriotism, national interest and national morale, quality of governance, political will, and character as complementary to others. We will ensure that we have these assets in place and stress asset optimization."

This is captured here because it is an action statement of commitment that agreed with the spirit and letters of the WaaGovernment book series. An inspired work, after reading, you are expected to rise and take action that will contribute to ending poverty in Africa. Yes, to end poverty in Africa, we must take personal development and patriotic actions very serious and engage in business ventures, trade, and services that promote the good of humanity as we commit to the enthronement of visionary leadership during an electioneering process in our communities, constituencies, States, and country.

It is known over the world that Africa is a land of plenty with over 60% of the world's uncultivated arable land and a population of 1.3 billion with millions of people of color in the Diaspora, the second biggest continent by landmass, and wealthiest continent in terms of the human and natural resource.

With these undisputed facts, Africa and Nigeria in particular should have no business with poverty. What the continent needs is a new set of leaders that think for the well-being of the people and the development of their community; Those who think for peace and improved standard of living of the citizenry.

We must be challenged to support only visionary leaders in positions of trust. Africa's underdevelopment is a question of leadership and patriotism. Despite government efforts, the GDP of African nations has continued to capsize for decades. Her per capita income has been embarrassingly low, compared to others. And according to Pastor Chris, "The answer lies in the fact that gross mental attitude is wrong. The answer lies in the fact that their gross mental output is horrendously low"

For a change, we must take action to end extreme poverty in our country. As stated earlier, poor mental attitude is the sole reason for underdevelopment in Africa and the reason for a naturally endowed continent that was the bedrock of civilization to be so backward in the world's scheme of things. Things must change, and there must be a landmark for change.

"Africa was always called a dark continent, not because of the color of their skin but because of the poverty of their minds. But the time has come for us to make a difference and we will."

According to Pastor Chris Oyakhilome, my mentor
and life coach.

And in this profound and painstaking 5 years of
detailed relationship-inspired classic work on
nation-building, patriotism, governance, and
Nationhood, you have been taking on a journey of
self and leadership development in this
revolutionary Classic, the book: TOWARDS A
BETTER COUNTRY: A QUEST FOR
VISIONARY LEADERSHIP IN AFRICA.

And the author believes you have been inspired
and trained to take action for the betterment of
your country. To stand in support of only visionary
leadership in your communities and consistency to
defend your right and to implement the knowledge
and inspiration you have been exposed to in this
work. By deciding to give vents for the flow of

passion ignited in you through the words and spirit embedded in this classic to be a Change in your country and to join hands with others to build our nations to become a better World.

With the new thinking, planted in the pages of this book, I believe that the African story must change. Africa is too blessed to be poor. Our environment is the envy of nations.

We don't have any business with poverty. We must come together, work together and change our thinking to change the African story forever.

Having been inspired, we must adopt the "See to succeed principle."

For example, we must See the blessings, the greatness the natural abundance, and how rich Nigeria and Africa are to contribute to a Change.

We must "See our vast arable virile lands for agriculture!

We must "See our viable best tourist hub sites all around the country!

We must "See a matching workforce of the population needed for the productive economy!

We must "See the abundant natural and human resources beyond measure"!

We must "See the size of our markets as an added advantage!

You must "See your potential, talents, and abilities, and decide to be another Dangote of Africa."

Nigeria is so blessed.

Any person can succeed in Nigeria.

But the question is, why on earth would Nigeria, a blessed country, be lagging in the comity of nations amid plenty? It happened because successive leaders failed. They pursue nationalism instead of nationhood.

And we are here to re-kindle hope with the WaaGovernment materials and to ignite the passion for a change in our quest for a better country that can only be possible when we have visionary leaders in the position of trust and governance.

In the new era envisaged for the greatness of our country, Nepotistic consideration, religious bigotry, and narrow thinking should have no place in the mind of the future leaders and citizens for a spring of hope and greatness of our Nation.

In Africa, Nigeria has the biggest market and remains the strongest economic force on the continent. Take advantage of the free environment and decide to be a success. Work with others. Become a uniting force and create a unity of purpose as the force of development in your community and city. Having passed the school of thought of this book, you must become the agent of change we need to advance in the comity of nations.

Corruption has badly affected the growth of our country, our citizens have suffered so much not because we don't have the resources to provide the basic social amenities in the country or a matching infrastructure for a productive economy but lack of Unity, visionary leadership and lack of loyalty to the country has been the bane of backwardness of the country. Having tried all along, with minimal results- No quality health system, very poor education funding, abysmally low investment in infrastructure, and a degradable environment in the Delta regions that plays vital roles in the nation's economy. Wisdom has demanded we set aside all religious and ethnic considerations and come together to build our country. And I think we should listen to the voice of wisdom and end extreme poverty and ignorance in our land.

Things must change. We must allow a competitive economy like that of the USA where all the component level of the federation is designed to be productive and competitive. We must put in place a system that checks corruption and accepts a less expensive system of government to favor people-oriented policies. These are made possible when we agree and design a "Well-thought restructured system that allows us to enhance productivity and boosts economic growth."

We must leverage our diversity and create regional markets to create enough jobs for our growing population. Each Region in the country must accept the political reconstruction of the country and the devolution of power to discourage laziness and over-dependence on the center. The Central and Unity system of government will not only kill the economic potential of our great country but would not also allow the building of trust in the system to drive prosperity and achieve nationhood.

We must set aside the corrupt system that threatens our country's unity and consciously put in place a framework that will stop regional crises and the incessant calls for secession. Politics against the political structures that will open up the system and provide equal rights for all Nigerians to strengthen the fabric that holds our beloved country together is a treasonable offense.

To get things working, there is a need for a strong collective desire and conviction to build our country beyond her fault lines. These are the integral parts of the new thinking enshrined in this classic and our campaign- the love for a country campaign designed for the achievement of a thriving state and nationhood in Africa.

I have caught the vision of this new thinking and in response; I am reaching out to you and to all stakeholders of Project Nigeria and lovers of Africa to stand up for a reformation in our country and a change in our continent. You must support the spread of the message in this book in your sphere of contact, In our schools, and in your community by standing in solidarity to make our country and continent great. The New Thinking, propounded in this inspired work, is the antidote needed to build a new country, productive economy, sustainable development, good governance, and nationhood in Africa for a prosperous continent and, peaceful egalitarian society.

Yes, with the actionable steps outlined in this classic work, WaaGovernment and Theory of Nations, on patriotism, nation-building, social change, good governance, and visionary leadership, we can win against poverty in Africa.

Yes, Africa can win with you!